Outdoor
ENTERTAINING

RECIPES AND FOOD STYLING

George Dolese

GENERAL EDITOR

Chuck Williams

PHOTOGRAPHY

Jim Franco

STYLING

Robin Turk

TEXT

Steve Siegelman

BONNIER
BOOKS

CONTENTS

THE ART OF ENTERTAINING OUTDOORS

Something remarkable happens when you entertain outdoors. Take away the walls and windows and suddenly everything changes. Food tastes different in the open air, surrounded by natural aromas and fresh breezes. The party flows freely and the conversation is lively. And nature serves up a first-class setting: blue skies on a spring morning, crickets singing on a summer night, the golden light of an autumn afternoon. With that kind of relaxed backdrop, you can't go wrong.

Of course, outdoor entertaining does present a few unique logistical challenges, such as keeping food hot or cold, coping with changes in the weather, and creating comfort in an open-air space. But it's also uniquely forgiving. As anyone who has been on a camping trip knows, even the simplest food seems to taste better when it's served outdoors, where a spirit of lighthearted improvisation prevails. Start with good food, add some flickering candles and a bit of colour to the table, and you'll be entertaining with ease.

That's the magic of an outdoor party. More than any other kind of gathering, it can be both creative and refreshingly casual at the same time, just the kind of low-stress affair we all want to host – and attend – these days. And whether you're planning a dinner on the patio, a chic cocktail party, a picnic at the beach, or a garden barbeque, this book is a good place to start.

It's filled with easy, outdoor-friendly menus, decorating ideas, and practical hosting and serving tips. Each chapter shows you how to create a complete party, but you can also mix and match recipes and ideas to plan an event that works for you. Either way, you'll find that outdoor entertaining is a no-fail proposition. The setting will do half the work for you, and your cooking and relaxed atmosphere will do the rest. Here's to great meals in the great outdoors.

OUTDOOR PARTY PLANNING

Whether it is a picnic, a casual dinner on the patio, or a brunch staged in the garden, the pleasure of sharing food with friends in the open air is irresistible. And with a little planning and organisation, outdoor entertaining can be even easier than hosting indoors. But it is different, and the recipes and ideas in this book have been designed with that difference in mind—from made-ahead, portable foods that work outdoors to strategies for lighting and setting the scene.

Choosing a Location

The weather is good and the occasion— a birthday celebration, a family reunion, a get-together with friends—feels right for an outdoor party. The first thing to decide is where to entertain. If you don't have space for outdoor entertaining, consider a casual picnic or even a more elaborate sit-down meal at a local park or beach. But if you have a backyard, patio, or garden, hosting at home is usually your best choice because you can prepare and serve the food from your own kitchen with minimal stress. You can make nearly any outdoor space work for entertaining, even a small terrace in the city. It's just a matter of matching the site with the right serving style and menu.

Serving Styles

Once you have decided on a location, you can begin to map out the logistics of the setting and choose a serving style that will work best. Start by addressing a few basic questions. How many guests? Will there be lots of kids? How casual or formal? Your goal should be to make your guests feel welcome and comfortable. No one expects you to put on an elaborate show, so let the hallmarks of outdoor entertaining—simplicity, ease, and fun—be your guiding principles as you envision how the meal will be served.

FAMILY-STYLE SERVICE, with platters and bowls of food passed at the table, works well for big, informal groups, especially if you are serving on a patio or other small space that does not allow for a separate buffet table. If your dining table is small, set up a side table, bench, or ledge to use as a sideboard for the platters.

BUFFET SERVICE is often the ideal choice for garden barbeques and big crowds. Set up one or more buffet stations for food and drinks with easy access on all sides. Small satellite dining tables are ideal for this kind of service because they can be placed in comfortable spots around the garden and easily moved to follow the shade or the sun.

RESTAURANT-STYLE SERVICE, with food arranged on individual plates in the kitchen, is well suited to an elegant multicourse meal. This serving style works best when

OUTDOOR ESSENTIALS

Keep a drawer, basket, or galvanized tub stocked with basic outdoor decorating and serving items for impromptu entertaining.

- A sturdy cotton tablecloth

- Disposable cocktail napkins in neutral tones to complement any colour scheme

- Candles (votives, pillars, and tapers) and candleholders; hurricane lamps or clear vases

- Strands of small white lights with twist ties for securing them

- Extension cords

- Paper lanterns

- Tiki torches, lamp oil, and extra wicks

- Citronella candles and insect repellent

- Small, unbreakable bowls and plates for snacks and dips

- Set of durable coasters

the dining table can be set up close to the kitchen. You may want to combine serving styles—for example, plating the salad or first course and dessert, and passing the main course and side dishes family style.

The Outdoor Menu

Outdoor entertaining is all about enjoying the warm days and evenings of spring, summer, and early autumn. It's a chance to serve casual food that makes the most of the fresh flavours and textures of seasonal produce. Use the recipes in this book for inspiration, and make a trip to a local farmer's market to find out which ingredients are at their peak.

The secret to successful entertaining outdoors is to serve mostly cold or room-temperature foods. Light, brightly flavoured cold dishes, such as salads, chilled soups, and simple, antipasto-style appetizers, are particularly refreshing when eaten outdoors. They are also portable, hold up well on the table or buffet, and require little last-minute attention from the host. For cocktail parties, use the same principle: mostly cold, self-serve food along with one or two hot passed appetizers.

A single hot item – generally the main course – accompanied by room-temperature dishes is all that it takes to make the meal feel substantial and satisfying. Grilling is an ideal way to achieve this balance without having to spend time in the kitchen during the party. If you plan a menu around a grilled main course, consider using the grill to cook one or more of the side dishes as well, such as corn on the cob or courgettes. The more that you can prepare in advance

and the less that you have to cook at the last minute, the more relaxed you'll be during the party and the more smoothly it will flow. A good rule of thumb is to choose recipes that are largely made ahead of time with only finishing touches needed just before the meal. Consider a do-it-yourself course, too, such as a make-your-own grilled sausage sandwich buffet or an ice-cream sundae bar. For desserts, think easy and light, such as a made-ahead cake or biscuits with fresh fruit or a granita or sorbet.

Give yourself a break and don't be overly ambitious. Outdoor food should be as uncomplicated as possible – easy to make, easy to serve, and easy to eat. Fresh seasonal ingredients, a light touch, and a little presentational style are all you need.

The Drinks

An outdoor party calls for fun, creative beverages, from sparkling wine and colourful cocktails to refreshing cool drinks. Greet your guests with an aperitif, such as Champagne, Prosecco, or Campari and soda, and serve it with salty snacks, like olives or nuts.

A signature mixed drink, whipped up in a cocktail shaker, is another ideal beverage choice. If you're not an experienced bartender, practice making the cocktail before the party, so that everything goes smoothly. Be sure to set out glassware that will show off the drink, and prepare a colourful garnish that complements whatever spirits you are using, such as a mint sprig, a twist of lemon peel, or chunks of fruit skewered on a cocktail stick. Always offer a nonalcoholic option as well.

For warm-weather daytime parties, set up a self-serve beverage station in a shady spot. Fill a galvanised tub with ice and pack it with white wine, beer, sodas, juices, and bottles of water. Stock the refrigerator with backups and replenish the tub as needed. Offer red wine at cool room temperature, and set out glassware, citrus wedges, ice, cocktail napkins, and a bottle opener.

Allow one litre of water and one bottle of wine for every two or three guests who drink. Buy bagged party ice, rather than relying on the trays in your freezer. Plan on at least 500 to 750 grams (1 to $1^1/_2$ lb) of ice per person, plus more if you will be chilling drinks in a tub. Have the ice delivered, or bring it home in a large cooler, where you can store it until you need it.

The Setting

One of the great advantages of entertaining outdoors is that when it comes to decorating and setting the scene, the location does most of the job for you. A few decorative accents are all that you need to add. Start with a simple idea – an Italian dinner, a homely barbeque, a tropical cocktail party, a special garden brunch – and let it guide you as you plan the look of the party.

Begin by making a basic diagram of the space and then work out where to put the dining table, seating, buffet, bar, and a drink station. Take into account whatever existing seating areas may be available, such as low walls, ledges, or terraces. For a sit-down meal, a seating chart can help to eliminate awkward decision making at the last minute. As you fill in your diagram, think about what kind of furniture will work best.

The Table

A comfortable table allows about two feet (60 cm) between the centre of one plate and the centre of the next. Think about your guest list, and decide if your outdoor table will easily accommodate everyone. If it is too small, you can bring out a larger table from indoors, rent a large folding table, or set up several small tables. Any sturdy table – even a weatherworn picnic table – can work well for outdoor entertaining. The day of the party, clean the table well and dress it with place mats, a tablecloth, or a centre mat and a simple natural centrepiece or decoration at each place setting that ties in with your party's theme and colour scheme.

For most parties, a table set with attractive everyday dishes, glassware, and flatware works well. Depending on your theme, you may want to add some outdoor-specific elements, like tin plates, bamboo-handled cutlery, rustic serving dishes, and linens or place mats with a heavy weave.

Keep table decorations unfussy and choose elements that relate to the setting. Make a centrepiece with flowers from your garden, or adorn each plate with a sprig of greenery from a nearby tree. You can also use herbs or seasonal fruits to decorate the table. Bring a touch of nature to a terrace with potted herbs and garden foliage, or dress up a table at the beach with islands of sand and shells. Whatever elements you choose, create a sense of unity with repeating patterns, such as a row of candles, uniformly folded napkins, and decorative matching place cards, and stay with a palette of no more than two or three colours.

Seating

When it comes to seating, you want your guests to feel as comfortable as they would at an indoor party. Add pillows to outdoor furniture, especially benches or hard wooden chairs. For a fancier look, use matching dining chairs or rent chairs from a party rental company. If renting, reserve chairs, cushions, and other supplies well in advance and have them delivered in plenty of time to allow for setup on the day of the party.

For picnics and casual garden parties, think creatively. Benches, hay bales, and driftwood logs can all work well, or you can lay out blankets or quilts in place of tables and use pillows for seating. To help delineate a seating area, set out a rug and arrange chairs or pillows around it.

Lighting

For any evening party, lighting is an effective way to set a mood. Remember that you are not only providing illumination, but also creating an inviting effect. Always be cautious of where you place candles.

GENERAL LIGHTING Before the party, work out a plan for illuminating the dining table, buffet, and bar. Assess how well existing outdoor lighting will do the job and whether you will need to supplement it with lanterns. Make sure pathways and stairs are well lit and extension cords are taped down and away from heavily trafficked areas.

MOOD LIGHTING Next, think about small lights that help set the mood. Use oil lamps or unscented votives or pillar candles in jars, tumblers, vases or hurricane lamps on the table, buffet, and bar. Wrap leaves around votives and secure with twine or tape for a decorative touch.

Add sparkle in the background with tiki torches, strands of tiny white lights, or hanging lanterns in trees and bushes, along the railing of a terrace, or intertwined in the spokes of a market umbrella over the table. Make luminarias by cutting decorative designs in small paper bags, filling them half full with sand, and placing a votive candle or small flashlight inside. If you have a pool or fountain, decorate it with floating candles.

Be generous in estimating how many candles you will need for the table and general decoration; you'll find that you can always use more. Buy bags of inexpensive tea lights, and keep extras on hand to restock throughout the evening. Make sure all candles and oil lamps are securely placed on solid surfaces where they won't be knocked over by guests or the wind.

Music

Give some thought to music ahead of time and choose a selection of songs that fit your theme. Set up a portable stereo or satellite speakers near your outdoor dining area. For large parties, let your neighbours know that you are expecting a crowd and when the event will begin and end – or better yet, invite them to join in the festivities.

Dealing with the Details

Of course, you and your guests will be counting on a warm, sunny day or a balmy evening, but have an alternative plan in case the weather changes. Think about how and where you can quickly restage the party indoors if the need arises. For picnics, pick an indoor alternative site ahead of time and include directions when you invite guests.

SUN For daytime parties, watch the path of the sun a few days in advance of your gathering to determine which areas will be comfortably shaded. If there are not enough shady spots, consider buying or renting one or more large market umbrellas to set up over the table or bar, or rent a canopy, or party tent.

WIND AND COLD If wind seems likely, be prepared with clothes pegs to secure the tablecloth, hurricane lamps to protect candles, and paperweights or rocks to hold down napkins. You might want to sew drapery weights into the hem of a tablecloth earmarked for outdoor entertaining. For glassware, use sturdy tumblers that won't blow over. Have throws, scarves, or sweaters on hand for guests who may need them as the weather cools down.

INSECTS Set out citronella candles to ward off mosquitoes and other insects, or use an electronic bug zapper. Have some natural insect repellent on hand for guests. Keep food covered until serving time, and if flies are a problem, use domed nets to cover platters, or rent small party tents to enclose the buffet and bar. Set pans of water under the legs of the table to keep away ants.

FOOD SAFETY Keep cold foods cold (no warmer than 4°C/40°F) in a cooler or refrigerator until just before you serve them, and then set them out in a shady spot. Keep hot foods hot (at least 60°C/140°F) with electric warmers or chafing dishes. If you're travelling to a location, transport the cooler inside the air-conditioned car, rather than the hot boot. For picnics, small cool packs are great inserts for baskets.

KIDS' STUFF If you are inviting families with children, designate a play area, and set out some outdoor toys and games, such as kites, bubble makers, beach balls, frisbees, and other sports equipment.

Finishing Touches

Outdoor entertaining is casual and relaxed. But even the most informal party can still have style and elegance. It's all a matter of preparing as much as you can in advance, making lists to stay organised, recruiting help when you need it, and adding a few creative touches to make the space and the food seem special. Use the recipes and ideas in this book as a starting point, and you'll discover just how easy it is to enjoy the simple pleasure of a meal shared with friends under the sun or the stars.

PICNIC ESSENTIALS

Stock a basket, cooler, or bin with picnic supplies so you're ready to picnic anytime, whether on a beach, at a sports event or concert, or on a blanket in the garden.

- Cling film for wrapping food, stacks of dishes, silverware, and other items
- Bags for depositing and transporting dirty dishes and serving ware
- Resealable plastic bags for leftovers
- Sharp knife, with the blade wrapped securely in cardboard for safe transport
- Lightweight plastic cutting board
- Corkscrew and bottle opener
- Serving spoons, forks, and salad servers
- Salt and pepper in resealable shakers
- Paper napkins, moist towelettes, and paper towels
- First-aid kit, ponchos, matches, candles, flashlights, tweezers, insect spray, and sunscreen

BEACHSIDE PICNIC DINNER

WORK PLAN

UP TO 1 DAY IN ADVANCE

Bake the biscuits and make the compote

Make the balsamic dipping oil

UP TO 12 HOURS IN ADVANCE

Prepare the soup

Prepare the salad and vinaigrette separately

Assemble the seafood cocktails

Mix the sangria

JUST BEFORE SERVING

Garnish the soup

Add the vinaigrette to the salad

HOSTING AND SERVING TIPS

- Cover a picnic table with a lightweight cotton or linen tablecloth or table mats.

- Lay a bed of sand along the centre of the table and decorate with shells, rocks, votives, or beach glass. On a windy day, arrange the objects directly on the table. Set votives in tall glass vases or hurricane lamps.

- Use clean seashells as salt and pepper cellars. Fill ahead and wrap in plastic.

- Repack store-bought foods (such as beverages or crisps) in attractive bottles and canisters or other containers.

- Bring an umbrella for shade and wind protection. Pack extra beach towels to drape over food until ready to serve.

MENU

Plum and Nectarine Sangria

Baguette Slices with Balsamic Dipping Oil

•

Cucumber Dill Soup

*Pepper, Tomato, Olive, and Manchego
Chopped Salad*

Layered Prawn and Crab Cocktail

•

*Strawberry Rhubarb Compote
with Brown Sugar Biscuits*

gather enough knives, forks, and spoons to make a set for each guest, and place each set in a napkin. Place knife blades facing inward for safe transportation.

fold each napkin around the cutlery, angling the folds slightly to create a pleasing effect. Wrap tightly to secure the cutlery.

tie each bundle with a piece of beach grass, twine, or string to hold it together. If desired, decorate with more strands of beach grass.

CUTLERY TO GO

Bundling cutlery in sturdy napkins makes transporting and serving easier and adds a decorative element to the table. Lay a bundle directly on the plate at each setting, or, if serving buffet style, stand the bundles upright in a small basket.

PLUM AND NECTARINE SANGRIA

Look for plums and nectarines that are ripe but still firm to ensure that they do not become too soft when soaked in the wine. Rinse the fruits well to remove any surface chemicals before slicing them. Use a dry white Rioja or Sauvignon Blanc for the wine.

In a large jug, combine the plum and nectarine wedges, nectarine nectar, orange liqueur, and white wine. Stir well, cover, and refrigerate for at least 2 hours or up to 12 hours to blend the flavours.

To serve, fill glasses with ice cubes and add the wine mixture, dividing evenly. Top off each glass with sparkling water. Serve at once.

Serves 6

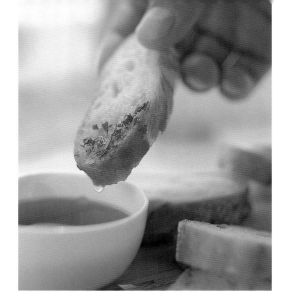

3 plums, halved, pitted, and cut into thin wedges

3 nectarines, halved, pitted, and cut into thin wedges

1 can (375 ml/12 fl oz) nectarine nectar

60 ml (2 fl oz) orange liqueur

1 bottle (750 ml/24 fl oz) dry white wine

Ice cubes

1 bottle (750 ml/24 fl oz) sparkling water, chilled

BAGUETTE SLICES WITH BALSAMIC DIPPING OIL

Quality olive oil and balsamic vinegar are essential to making this otherwise simple recipe into something special. Look for a green olive oil with a full flavour and a balsamic vinegar aged for at least three years.

160 ml (5 fl oz) extra-virgin olive oil

80 ml (3 fl oz) aged balsamic vinegar

1 teaspoon chopped fresh rosemary

In a small bowl, stir together the olive oil, vinegar, rosemary, garlic, lemon zest, and red pepper flakes. Cover and set aside at room temperature for at least 30 minutes or up to 24 hours to blend the flavours.

1 clove garlic, finely chopped

1 teaspoon finely grated lemon zest

Pinch of red pepper flakes

1 baguette, thinly sliced on the diagonal

To serve, pour the dipping oil into a small, shallow bowl and arrange the baguette slices on a board alongside.

Serves 6

CUCUMBER DILL SOUP

3 cucumbers, peeled, halved lengthwise, and seeded

250 g (8 oz) Greek-style or other thick, whole-milk plain yogurt

1 tablespoon fresh lemon juice

3 spring onions, including tender green tops, chopped

3 tablespoons chopped fresh dill

1 clove garlic, chopped

1 teaspoon caraway seeds, crushed

1 teaspoon sea salt

1/4 teaspoon ground white pepper

250 ml (8 fl oz) vegetable stock

2 tablespoons fruity extra-virgin olive oil

A chilled soup is a great beginning for a picnic at the beach or on a boat. For foolproof transport, select a container with a tight-fitting lid that permits easy pouring. Pour in the soup, cap tightly, place upright in an ice chest, and secure in place with bags of ice or cool packs. To serve, pour the soup into widemouthed glasses or cups so that guests can sip it.

Coarsely chop 5 of the cucumber halves and transfer to a large bowl. Add the yogurt, lemon juice, spring onions, dill, garlic, caraway seeds, salt, and white pepper. Stir to combine, cover with plastic wrap, and set aside at room temperature for 1 hour to blend the flavours. Dice the remaining cucumber half and set aside until ready to serve.

In a blender, purée the cucumber mixture until smooth. With the machine running, slowly add the stock and purée until it is fully incorporated, about 30 seconds. Transfer to a jug, cover with cling film, and refrigerate until chilled, about 2 hours. (The soup can be prepared up to 12 hours in advance and stored in an airtight container in the refrigerator. If it separates, simply stir it until emulsified.)

Just before serving, stir in the diced cucumber and olive oil. Pour the soup into widemouthed glasses or cups and serve at once.

Serves 6

Pepper, Tomato, Olive, and Manchego Chopped Salad

Chopped salads taste best when made a couple of hours before serving, so that the various flavours have time to blend. Use vegetables that have some crunch, such as those listed here, or cucumbers, fennel, and carrots. For a more substantial salad, add 185 g (6 oz) diced ham or dry salami.

To make the vinaigrette, in a large salad bowl, whisk together the olive oil, vinegar, mustard, garlic, salt, and pepper.

Add the peppers, tomatoes, celery, olives, onion, parsley, thyme, and cheese to the vinaigrette in the bowl. Toss until all the ingredients are coated with the vinaigrette. Transfer to an airtight container and refrigerate for up to 2 hours before serving. (The vegetables for the salad can be prepared up to 12 hours in advance and refrigerated. You can mix the vinaigrette at the same time and then combine it with the salad a couple of hours before serving.)

Serves 6

VINAIGRETTE

60 ml (2 fl oz) olive oil

3 tablespoons sherry vinegar

1 teaspoon Dijon mustard

1 clove garlic, minced

$1/4$ teaspoon sea salt

$1/2$ teaspoon freshly ground pepper

1 small yellow pepper (capsicum), seeded and diced

1 small orange pepper (capsicum), seeded and diced

375 g (12 oz) cherry tomatoes or plum tomatoes, stems removed and halved

4 celery stalks, thinly sliced

90 g (3 oz) pitted large Spanish green olives, quartered

45 g ($1^{1}/_{2}$ oz) finely chopped red onion

1 tablespoon chopped fresh flat-leaf (Italian) parsley

1 teaspoon chopped fresh thyme

250 g ($1/2$ lb) Manchego cheese, cut into 6 mm ($1/4$ inch) cubes

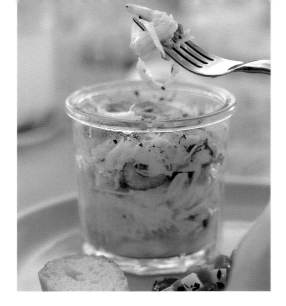

LAYERED PRAWN AND CRAB COCKTAIL

Individually packed jars make serving shellfish outside easy. The cocktails can be prepared up to twelve hours ahead and stored in the refrigerator. Use ice packs for transport and keep the cocktails cold until ready to serve. Look for ready-to-serve prawns and crabmeat at seafood counters.

To make the vinaigrette, in a small bowl, whisk together the olive oil, lemon zest, lemon juice, mustard, garlic, oregano, and saffron. Season to taste with salt and pepper.

Wash and thoroughly dry six 375 ml (12 fl oz) canning jars with glass lids. Place half of the prawns in the bottoms of the 6 jars, dividing them evenly. Top with half of the celery, spring onions, crabmeat, and fennel slices. Repeat the layers, starting with the prawns and finishing with the fennel slices. Drizzle the vinaigrette into the jars, dividing it evenly. Garnish the top of each jar with a lemon slice and a bay leaf. Close the lids and refrigerate the jars for 2 hours or up to 12 hours to blend the flavours.

Just before serving, rock each jar back and forth a few times to distribute the vinaigrette. Serve cold directly from the jars.

Serves 6

VINAIGRETTE

180 ml (6 fl oz) olive oil

Grated zest of 1 lemon

60 ml (2 fl oz) fresh lemon juice

1 teaspoon Dijon mustard

1 clove garlic, finely chopped

2 teaspoons chopped fresh oregano

Pinch of saffron threads

sea salt and freshly ground pepper

SEAFOOD COCKTAIL

500 g (1 lb) peeled cooked prawns

3 celery stalks, thinly sliced

3 spring onions, including tender green tops, chopped

500 g (1 lb) crabmeat, picked over for shell fragments

1 fennel bulb, trimmed, quartered lengthwise, cored, and sliced crosswise paper-thin

6 thin lemon slices

6 small bay leaves

Strawberry Rhubarb Compote with Brown Sugar Biscuits

Make this cool compote of summer fruits and these crisp biscuits a day in advance to keep your last-minute to-do list at a minimum.

To make the compote, in a nonreactive saucepan over medium-high heat, combine the rhubarb, strawberries, butter, brown sugar, granulated sugar, vanilla pod, and lemon zest and juice. Bring to a boil, stirring gently, and then reduce the heat to low. Simmer until the fruits are soft, 10-12 minutes. Allow to cool and then discard the vanilla pod. Transfer the cooled compote to an airtight container and refrigerate. (The compote can be prepared up to 1 day in advance.)

To make the biscuits, in a bowl, sift together the flour, baking soda, cloves, ginger, and salt. Set aside. In a food processor fitted with the paddle attachment, cream the butter and brown sugar on medium-high speed until smooth, about 3 minutes. Slowly stream in the maple syrup and continue to beat until well incorporated, about 2 minutes longer. Reduce the speed to low and add the flour mixture 75 g ($2^{1}/_2$ oz) at a time. Continue beating until the mixture comes together into a dough, about 3 minutes. Transfer the dough to a lightly floured work surface, divide it in half, and form each half into a disk 15 cm (6 in) in diameter. Wrap each disk in cling film and refrigerate for 1 hour.

Position a rack in the middle of the oven and a second rack in the upper third and preheat to 180°C (350°F). Line two 30 by 43 cm (12 by 17 in) baking sheets with parchment (baking) paper. On a lightly floured work surface, roll out 1 dough disk into an oval about 12 mm ($^{1}/_2$ in) thick. Transfer the dough to a prepared baking sheet and continue to roll until it is 3 mm ($^{1}/_8$ in) thick. Sprinkle 1 tablespoon of the coarse sugar evenly over the surface. Repeat with the second dough disk.

Bake until firm and brittle, about 20 minutes, alternating the pans between the 2 oven racks after the first 10 minutes of baking time. Let them cool on a wire rack. (Once cool, the cookies can be wrapped and stored at room temperature for up to 1 day.)

To serve, spoon the compote into individual bowls. Break 1 biscuit into 12 pieces and garnish each bowl with 2 pieces. Pass the second biscuit, allowing guests to break off pieces.

Serves 6

COMPOTE

6 stalks rhubarb, about 655 g ($1^{1}/_3$ lb) total weight, cut crosswise into 12 mm ($^{1}/_2$ in) pieces

250 g (8 oz) strawberries, hulled and quartered

3 tablespoons unsalted butter

105 g ($3^{1}/_2$ oz) firmly packed light brown sugar

125 g (4 oz) granulated sugar

1 vanilla pod, split lengthwise

Finely grated zest and juice of 1 lemon

BROWN SUGAR BISCUITS

390 g ($12^{1}/_2$ oz) plain flour

2 teaspoons baking soda (bicarbonate of soda)

1 teaspoon ground cloves

1 teaspoon ground ginger

$^{3}/_4$ teaspoon salt

250 g (8 oz) unsalted butter, at room temperature

280 g (9 oz) firmly packed light brown sugar

105 ml ($3^{1}/_2$ fl oz) maple syrup

2 tablespoons coarse sugar crystals

ELEGANT GARDEN BRUNCH

HOSTING AND SERVING TIPS

- Set up the table where it will remain in dappled shade.

- Select linens and tableware in a palette of off-whites and pale pastels, and use glass jugs and parfait dishes to add sparkle.

- Decorate the table with flowers from the garden, or purchase flowers with a homegrown look.

- Decorate the napkins with flower buds and lavender sprigs.

- Plate food in the kitchen and carry it to the table on linen-lined trays.

- For wine, serve a Beaujolais Nouveau or Lambrusco for a red and a sparkling wine for a white.

MENU

Apple Limeade

·

*Fresh Fruit, Honey, and
Yogurt Muesli Parfaits*

*Breakfast Bruschetta with Tomato,
Eggs, and Pancetta*

Frisée and Watercress Salad

·

Lemon Ring Cake

WORK PLAN

UP TO 12 HOURS IN ADVANCE
Mix the limeade

Bake the cake

UP TO 4 HOURS IN ADVANCE
Make the vinaigrette

Ready the salad greens

Prepare the parfaits

JUST BEFORE SERVING
Garnish the parfaits

Make the breakfast bruschetta

Dress the salad

Garden Flower Centrepiece

A simple centrepiece made with flowers from the garden ties the table and the setting together, creating a harmonious look. If roses are not available, use other delicately coloured blooms, such as peonies, lilacs, or dahlias.

snip two to three dozen blossoms in your garden. Trim off all but a few leaves from each stem.

select a clear glass vase that will catch and reflect light. Place clear marbles or stones in the bottom. Fill with lukewarm water to just above the level of the stones.

arrange the flowers in the vase, pushing the stems between the stones to secure them. Keep the arrangement low, so it won't block sight lines.

Apple Limeade

*To vary this quick and refreshing morning drink, add 15 g (¹/₂ oz)
fresh mint leaves or 1 tablespoon peeled and finely grated fresh ginger
to the juice mixture before refrigerating.*

Cut 10 of the limes in half and squeeze the juice from them. You should have
about 250 ml (8 fl oz) juice. Reserve 6 squeezed lime halves and discard the rest.
In a large glass jar or jug, combine the lime juice, apple juice, and the reserved
squeezed lime halves. Cover and refrigerate for at least 1 hour or up to 12 hours to
blend the flavours.

When ready to serve, cut the remaining 2 limes into 6 slices each. Fill a large
serving pitcher half full with ice and add the sparkling water, lime slices, and apple
slices. Strain the apple juice mixture through a fine-mesh sieve into the jug and stir.
Pour into tall chilled glasses over ice and serve at once.

Serves 6

12 limes

1 litre (32 fl oz) unfiltered
cold-pressed apple juice

Ice cubes

1 bottle (750 ml/24 fl oz) sparkling
water

2 small Granny Smith apples, halved,
cored, and sliced

Fresh Fruit, Honey, and Yogurt Muesli Parfaits

*Here, layers of fresh berries and creamy yogurt served in parfait glasses
signal the start of a leisurely brunch. If Greek-style yogurt, which is
thicker than most yogurts, is unavailable, use plain whole-milk yogurt.*

For each parfait, place 3 tablespoons of the berries in the bottom of a tall parfait
glass. Top with 3 tablespoons of the yogurt and drizzle with 2 teaspoons of the
honey. Repeat the berry and yogurt layers. Cover each glass loosely with plastic
wrap and refrigerate for up to 4 hours. To serve, top each parfait with 3 fig wedges
and a few berries and sprinkle with 2 tablespoons of the muesli. Drizzle each with
1 tablespoon honey and serve at once.

Serves 6

315 g (10 oz) mixed berries such as
blackberries, raspberries, and
blueberries, plus more for garnish

625 g (1¹/₄ lb) Greek-style or other
thick, whole-milk plain yogurt

90 g (3 oz) honey, plus
6 tablespoons 125 g (4 oz) for drizzling

185 g (6 oz) grain-and-nut muesli

3 figs, each cut into 6 wedges

Breakfast Bruschetta with Tomato, Eggs, and Pancetta

Scrambled eggs become something special when beaten with a little crème fraîche and topped with summer tomatoes and crispy curls of pancetta. If you have some truffle oil on hand, use it in place of the extra-virgin olive oil.

6 slices French bread

2 tablespoons olive oil

6 thin slices pancetta

185 g (6 oz) cherry tomatoes

1/2 teaspoon sea salt

1/4 teaspoon freshly ground pepper

SCRAMBLED EGGS

8 large eggs

90 g (3 oz) crème fraîche

10 g (1/3 oz) snipped fresh chives, plus extra for garnish

1/2 teaspoon sea salt

3 tablespoons unsalted butter

Parmesan cheese shavings for garnish

Fruity extra-virgin olive oil for drizzling

Position a rack 15 cm (6 in) from the heat source and preheat the grill.

Lightly brush both sides of each bread slice with the olive oil and arrange on a rimmed baking sheet. Place the bread under the grill and toast until the edges start to turn golden, about 30 seconds. Turn the slices over and toast until the second side is golden, about 30 seconds longer. Wrap the toasted bread in aluminium foil and keep warm until ready to serve.

Arrange each pancetta slice in a single layer on a separate rimmed baking sheet. Place under the grill and grill until the edges start to curl and turn brown, about 2 minutes. Wrap the pancetta in foil and keep warm until ready to serve.

Slice the tomatoes in half through the stem end and place them in a bowl. Sprinkle with the salt and pepper and toss to season evenly. Set aside.

To make the scrambled eggs, in a large bowl, beat together the eggs, crème fraîche, 10 g (1/3 oz) chives, and salt. In a large nonstick sauté pan over medium heat, melt the butter, add the egg mixture, and let cook undisturbed for about 1 minute to warm through. Using a silicone spatula, gently turn over areas of the eggs as they set, then fold and stir them into soft and slighty runny curds, 1-2 minutes longer.

To serve, place a slice of toasted bread on each individual plate. Top each bread slice with some of the scrambled eggs and tomatoes. Garnish with a pancetta curl, Parmesan shavings, a drizzle of extra-virgin olive oil, and a sprinkle of chives. Serve at once.

Serves 6

Frisée and Watercress Salad

Crisp and refreshing, a simple well-dressed side salad makes a good plate partner for the breakfast bruschetta (page 42). This salad can be transformed into a more elaborate first course by garnishing it with a few toasted walnut halves and some crumbled blue or goat cheese.

To make the vinaigrette, in a small bowl, whisk together the shallot, olive oil, walnut oil, vinegar, and mustard. Season to taste with salt and pepper. Let stand at room temperature for at least 30 minutes or up to 4 hours to blend the flavours.

Remove the tough outer leaves from the frisée and discard. Tear the remainder of the leaves into 5 cm (2 in) pieces and rinse with the watercress under cold water in a colander to remove any soil. Dry the leaves and transfer them to a large salad bowl. Add the cucumber slices. Place a slightly damp paper towel over the top, cover with plastic wrap, and refrigerate until ready to serve, up to 4 hours in advance.

When ready to serve, toss the prepared salad with the vinaigrette.

Serves 6

VINAIGRETTE

1 shallot, finely chopped

60 ml (2 fl oz) olive oil

3 tablespoons walnut oil

2 tablespoons Champagne vinegar

1/2 teaspoon Dijon mustard

Sea salt and freshly ground pepper

1 head frisée

1 bunch watercress, stemmed

1/2 cucumber, thinly sliced

LEMON RING CAKE

375 g (12 oz) plain flour

2 teaspoons baking powder

1 teaspoon salt

375 g (12 oz) unsalted butter, at room temperature

250 g (^{1}/$_2$ lb) cream cheese, at room temperature

500 g (1 lb) sugar

6 large eggs

2 teaspoons vanilla extract (essence)

1 tablespoon finely grated lemon zest

60 ml (2 fl oz) fresh lemon juice

LEMON SYRUP

1 tablespoon finely grated lemon zest

125 ml (4 fl oz) fresh lemon juice

125 g (4 oz) sugar

315 g (10 oz) lemon curd or marmalade (optional)

Lemon slices for garnish

Take advantage of the fact that this cake holds beautifully, and prepare it the evening before. When serving, place a bowl of lemon curd or marmalade in the centre of a platter and surround with cake wedges.

Preheat the oven to 180°C (350°F). Lightly butter a 2.5 litre (2^1/$_2$ qt) Bundt pan. Dust with flour and tap out the excess. In a large bowl, sift together the flour, baking powder, and salt. Set aside.

In a food processor fitted with the paddle attachment, cream together the butter and cream cheese on medium-high speed until smooth, about 3 minutes. Reduce the speed to medium and add the sugar. Continue to beat until light and fluffy, about 2 minutes longer. Beat in the eggs one at a time, beating well after each addition. Remove the bowl from the mixer and, using a rubber spatula, fold in the flour mixture until incorporated. Stir in the vanilla, lemon zest, and lemon juice.

Pour the batter into the prepared mould and smooth the top with the spatula. Bake until a skewer inserted in the centre comes out clean, about 1 hour. Transfer to a wire rack and allow to cool in the pan for 30 minutes.

While the cake is baking, make the lemon syrup: In a nonreactive saucepan over medium heat, combine the lemon zest, lemon juice, and sugar, stirring until the sugar is dissolved. Bring to a boil and then reduce the heat to low. Simmer until reduced by one-third, 10-15 minutes. Remove from the heat and allow to stand at room temperature until ready to use.

To loosen the cake, tap the sides of the mould gently on the worktop. Invert a flat cake plate or pedestal over the pan and invert the plate and the pan together. Tap the bottom of the pan with your hand and then lift off the pan. While the cake is still warm, poke holes in the surface with a skewer and brush the cake all over with the lemon syrup, allowing the cake to absorb the syrup before applying more. Let the cake cool for 30 minutes longer before serving. (The cake can be baked and glazed up to 12 hours in advance. Allow to cool to room temperature and tent loosely with cling film.)

Just before serving, slice the cake into wedges and garnish with lemon slices. Serve alongside a bowl of lemon curd or marmalade, if desired.

Serves 6

ITALIAN FAMILY-STYLE DINNER

HOSTING AND SERVING TIPS

- Create an edible centrepiece: Arrange olives, grape clusters, and country-style bread with olive oil and vinegar for dipping on a wooden cutting board.

- Start with an easy antipasto platter of Italian meats, marinated mushrooms or artichoke hearts, and chunks of Parmesan cheese.

- Serve wine in carafes. Fill a galvanized bucket with ice and an assortment of water and soft drinks.

- Garnish platters with grape, citrus, fig, or other nontoxic leaves.

- For wine, serve a light Sangiovese or Valpolicella for a red and a Pinot Grigio or Vermentino for a white.

MENU

Caprese Salad

Tuna and Farro Salad

Rosemary-Sage Pork Tenderloin
with Pancetta and Fried Capers

Roasted Cauliflower with Green Olives

•

Cappuccino Granita

Amaretto Cordials

WORK PLAN

UP TO 2 DAYS IN ADVANCE
Make the granita

UP TO 1 DAY IN ADVANCE
Roast the pork loin and cauliflower

UP TO 4 HOURS IN ADVANCE
Prepare the *farro* salad,
keeping the radicchio separate

JUST BEFORE SERVING
Make the caprese salad

Add the radicchio to the *farro* salad

Finish the pork and cauliflower

Assemble the granita and mix the cordials

VOTIVE PLACE CARDS

Twinkling candles set in glasses do double duty as place cards, welcoming each guest with a warm glow. As the sun goes down, they stay lit beside each place setting, providing extra illumination and adding to the Italian countryside mood.

gather glass tumblers or stocky glasses, tea lights or votives, twine or ribbon, decorative name cards, and grape leaves or other seasonal foliage.

place a candle in each glass. Write a guest's name on each card. Punch a small hole in the card and the leaf, and thread them together on the twine.

tie a place card around each glass and set a finished votive on each plate. Light the candles just before the guests are seated.

CAPRESE SALAD

Tomatoes filled with mozzarella slices and basil leaves make for a beautiful presentation and are easy to serve. Balsamic glaze, which is used to season the salad, is found alongside the balsamic vinegars in many stores. If unavailable, use a well-aged balsamic vinegar.

Place the tomatoes on a cutting board, stem side down. Using a sharp knife, make 4 evenly spaced slits crosswise in each tomato, stopping about 12 mm ($^1/_2$ in) from the bottom.

Cut the mozzarella into 32 thin, uniform slices. Working with 1 tomato at a time, insert 1 mozzarella slice and 1 basil leaf into each slit.

When ready to serve, place the prepared tomatoes on a platter. Drizzle with the olive oil and balsamic glaze and season with the salt and pepper. Serve at once.

Serves 8

8 tomatoes

4 balls fresh mozzarella cheese, about 375 g ($^3/_4$ lb) total weight

32 fresh basil leaves

Extra-virgin olive oil for drizzling

Balsamic vinegar glaze for drizzling

Sea salt and freshly ground pepper

Tuna and Farro Salad

330 g (10½ oz) *farro*, soaked in water to cover for 20 minutes and drained

VINAIGRETTE

80 ml (3 fl oz) olive oil

2 tablespoons red wine vinegar

2 tablespoons fresh lemon juice

4 teaspoons brined-cured green peppercorns, chopped

½ teaspoon sea salt

330 g (10½ oz) Italian tuna packed in olive oil, drained and flaked

½ white onion, finely diced

1 celery stalk, thinly sliced

15 g (½ oz) coarsely chopped fresh flat-leaf (Italian) parsley

1 clove garlic, finely chopped

Sea salt and freshly ground pepper

1 small head radicchio, julienned

Lemon wedges for garnish

Extra-virgin olive oil for drizzling

Farro, an ancient wheat that is similar to spelt and is a speciality of Tuscany and Umbria, makes an excellent salad because it maintains its shape and texture. It is sold in Italian speciality-food stores and health-food markets. Whole-wheat (wholemeal) couscous or short-grain brown rice makes a good substitute.

In a large saucepan over high heat, combine the *farro* with 1.5 litres (48 fl oz) water and bring to a boil. Reduce the heat to medium-low, cover, and simmer until the grains are tender but not soft, about 30 minutes. Pour into a colander, rinse with cold water, and set aside to drain.

To make the vinaigrette, in a large salad bowl, whisk together the olive oil, vinegar, lemon juice, peppercorns, and salt.

Add the *farro*, tuna, onion, celery, parsley, and garlic to the vinaigrette and toss until evenly coated. Season to taste with salt and pepper. (The salad can be prepared up to 4 hours in advance, covered with cling film, and stored at cool room temperature.)

To serve, add the radicchio to the salad bowl and toss to combine. Garnish with the lemon wedges and drizzle with a little extra-virgin olive oil. Serve at once.

Serves 8

ROSEMARY-SAGE PORK TENDERLOIN WITH PANCETTA AND FRIED CAPERS

Saturated with the flavours of rosemary and sage, these pork tenderloins are a quick interpretation of the popular porchetta *found throughout Tuscany and are served at room temperature. Leftover pork can be used in sandwiches or salads.*

In a small bowl, combine the olive oil, rosemary, sage, fennel seeds, sea salt, and pepper and mix well. Using the tip of a sharp paring knife, make 8 crosswise incisions 12 mm (¹/₂ in) deep evenly spaced along the length of each tenderloin. Insert a garlic quarter into each incision. Rub the rosemary-sage mixture over the tenderloins. Wrap 2 slices of pancetta around each of the tenderloins in a spiral pattern. Place the tenderloins, side by side, in a baking dish. Cover tightly with plastic wrap and refrigerate for at least 24 hours or up to 2 days.

Remove the pork from the refrigerator and allow to stand at room temperature for about 1 hour before roasting. Preheat the oven to 190°C (375°F).

Transfer the tenderloins to a small roasting pan and pat dry with paper towels. Roast until an instant-read thermometer inserted into the thickest part registers 65°C (150°F), about 30 minutes. Let it cool to room temperature. Remove the pancetta slices and finely chop them. Set aside. (The pork can be prepared up to this point 1 day in advance. If doing so, cover with cling film and refrigerate along with the chopped pancetta until 30 minutes before serving.)

To fry the capers, in a bowl, toss the capers with the cornmeal until lightly coated. In a nonstick frying pan over high heat, warm the olive oil. When it is hot, drop in the capers and fry until golden, 1-2 minutes. Using a slotted spoon, transfer to a plate lined with a paper towel to drain. Lightly sprinkle the capers with sea salt.

To serve, thinly slice the pork and arrange on a serving platter. Scatter the fried capers and pancetta over the pork slices.

Serves 8

1 tablespoon olive oil

2 tablespoons chopped fresh rosemary

2 tablespoons chopped fresh sage

1 tablespoon fennel seeds, crushed

1¹/₂ teaspoons sea salt

¹/₂ teaspoon freshly ground pepper

2 pork tenderloins, trimmed,
about 750 g (1¹/₂ lb) total weight

4 cloves garlic, quartered lengthwise

4 thin slices pancetta

FRIED CAPERS

60 g (2 oz) capers, drained
and patted dry

1 tablespoon fine cornmeal or polenta

125 ml (4 fl oz) olive oil

Sea salt

Roasted Cauliflower with Green Olives

1 large head cauliflower,
about 1 kg (2 lb)

125 g (4 oz) pitted large green
olives, quartered

60 ml (2 fl oz) olive oil

1/4 teaspoon sea salt

1/4 teaspoon freshly ground pepper

2 tablespoons chopped fresh flat-leaf
(Italian) parsley

45 g (1/2 oz) store-bought seasoned
croutons, ground to crumbs in a
food processor

This dish tastes best at room temperature, making it ideal for entertaining. To save preparation time, look for large green olives that have already been pitted. They can be found prepacked in glass jars or purchased by weight from most supermarket olive bars.

Preheat the oven to 200°C (400°F). Lightly oil a nonstick rimmed baking sheet, approximate size 30 by 43 cm (12 by 17 in).

Cut the cauliflower head in half, slicing through the core. Using a sharp paring knife, remove the core from each half and discard. Cut the cauliflower into small florets, each about 12 mm ($^1/_2$ in) in diameter.

In a bowl, combine the cauliflower, olives, olive oil, salt, and pepper and toss until the cauliflower and olives are evenly coated. Transfer to the prepared baking sheet and spread in a single layer. Roast the cauliflower and olives for 10 minutes. Stir to toss and continue to roast until the florets are lightly golden, 10-12 minutes longer. Remove from the oven. Sprinkle with the parsley and bread crumbs and toss to combine. Allow to cool to room temperature. (The cauliflower and olives can be roasted up to 1 day in advance, covered, refrigerated, and brought to room temperature before serving.)

To serve, mound the cauliflower and olives in the centre of a platter or shallow serving bowl.

Serves 8

CAPPUCCINO GRANITA

Simple and elegant, this refreshing granita should be made at least twelve hours ahead so that the ice crystals are frozen solid. Serve with store-bought amaretto cookies in their decorative wrapping papers.

In a large bowl, combine the coffee, sugar, and cinnamon and stir until the sugar is dissolved. Whisk in 60 ml (2 fl oz) of the cream and chill for about 30 minutes. Pour the mixture into a shallow gratin dish and place in the freezer. Using a fork, scrape around the sides of the dish every 30 minutes to break up the ice crystals until all the liquid is completely frozen, about 3 hours. Cover tightly with cling film and keep frozen until ready to serve. (The granita can be prepared up to 2 days in advance and stored in the freezer.)

Just before serving, using a handheld mixer, whip the remaining 250 ml (8 fl oz) cream on medium-high speed until soft peaks form, about 3 minutes. Divide the granita between 8 coffee cups with saucers. Top each cup with a dollop of whipped cream and a sprinkle of chocolate shavings. Place an amaretto biscuit alongside each cup and serve at once.

Serves 8

1 litre (32 fl oz) freshly brewed double-strength coffee

125 g (4 oz) sugar

2 teaspoons ground cinnamon

310 ml (10 fl oz) double cream

Plain chocolate shavings for garnish

8 store-bought amaretto biscuits in wrappers for serving

AMARETTO CORDIALS

After-dinner cordials are traditionally served after the coffee. Instead, offer your guests this iced drink to sip while eating their granita.

Put 8 cordial glasses in the freezer to chill for at least 30 minutes. Fill a cocktail shaker half full with ice. Pour in the amaretto and cherry syrup. Cover with the lid and shake vigorously up and down for 10 seconds. Strain into the chilled glasses, dividing evenly. Garnish each glass with a maraschino cherry. Serve at once.

Serves 8

Ice cubes

375 ml (12 fl oz) amaretto liqueur

125 ml (4 fl oz) cherry-flavoured (Italian) syrup

8 maraschino cherries with stems

POOLSIDE COCKTAIL PARTY

HOSTING AND SERVING TIPS

- Set up a bar near the pool with sparkling and still water, beer, wine, soft drinks, juice, and plenty of ice.

- Pass finger-food appetizers that can be easily eaten in one or two bites.

- Round out the menu with salty snacks, such as pistachios or gourmet crisps.

- Use tall outdoor candles or tiki torches to tie the setting together.

- Decorate trays with tropical foliage, such as ti leaves and orchids.

- For wine, serve a medium-bodied Zinfandel for a red and a dry Riesling or Chardonnay for a white.

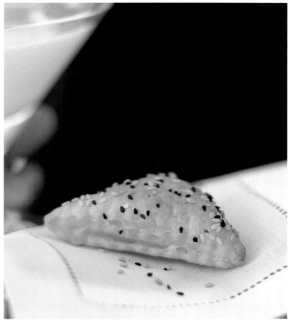

MENU

Key Lime Vodka Freezes

Sparkling Ginger Coolers

•

Sesame Seed Puffs

Curried Chicken and Mango Cocktail Tartlets

Beef Kebabs with Basil-Pesto Dipping Sauce

Prawn, Cantaloupe, and Fresh Herb Kebabs

•

Assorted Fruit Sorbet Shots

WORK PLAN

UP TO 1 WEEK IN ADVANCE

Make the ginger syrup

UP TO 1 DAY IN ADVANCE

Prepare the Key lime mixture

Bake the sesame seed puffs

Make the dipping sauce and marinate the beef

Prepare the chicken topping and toast the naan bread

Prepare and freeze the sorbet shots

4 TO 12 HOURS IN ADVANCE

Prepare the prawn kebabs

JUST BEFORE SERVING

Assemble the tartlets

Cook the beef kebabs

Garnish the sorbet shots

Mix the cocktails

select postcards that match your colour scheme or party theme, and cut them into squares using scissors, a utility knife, or a paper cutter.

print copies of the menu on your computer. Include crop marks to aid in trimming. Cut each menu to the size of the postcard squares.

attach the menus to the backs of the postcards using double-sided tape, spray adhesive, or a glue stick. Welcome each guest with a coaster and a cocktail.

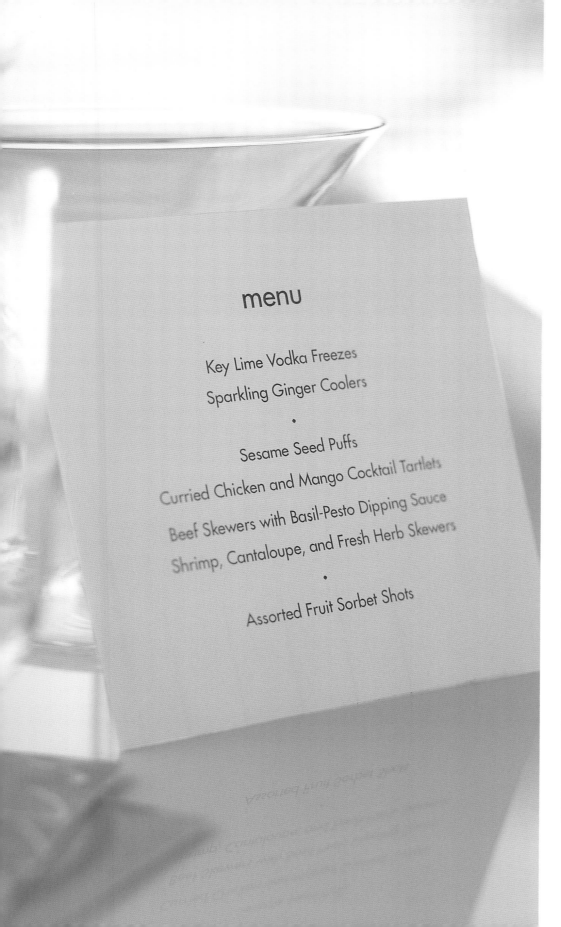

menu

Key Lime Vodka Freezes
Sparkling Ginger Coolers

·

Sesame Seed Puffs

Curried Chicken and Mango Cocktail Tartlets
Beef Skewers with Basil-Pesto Dipping Sauce
Shrimp, Cantaloupe, and Fresh Herb Skewers

·

Assorted Fruit Sorbet Shots

MENU COASTERS

*Colourful double-sided coasters,
with the party menu on one side,
are a fun way to give your guests
a preview of the food and drinks
you will be serving. Make one
coaster per guest, plus a few extras.*

KEY LIME VODKA FREEZES

Use fresh lime juice for the best results. Look for Key limes in speciality food stores or markets.

In a large jug, stir together the vodka, lime juice, and ginger syrup. Cover and refrigerate until ready to serve or for up to 1 day.

Chill 12 martini glasses in the freezer for at least 30 minutes. When ready to serve, mix in 3 batches: Fill a cocktail shaker half full with ice, pour in one-third of the drink mixture, cover, and shake vigorously for 10 seconds. Strain into 4 of the chilled glasses, garnish each with a lime slice, and serve. Repeat to make 2 more batches.

Serves 12

750 ml (24 fl oz) vodka

180 ml (6 fl oz) fresh
Key lime juice

375 ml (12 fl oz)
ginger syrup (below)

Ice cubes

12 Key lime slices

SPARKLING GINGER COCKTAILS

Flavoured sugar syrups, such as the homemade ginger syrup used here for this non-alcoholic cooler, dress up both hot and cold beverages. Keep a few store-bought Italian-style flavoured syrups on hand for last-minute entertaining.

To make the ginger syrup, in a saucepan over low heat, combine the water, sugar, fresh ginger, vanilla pod, and cloves. Stir until the sugar is dissolved and the syrup is infused with flavour, about 10 minutes. Remove from the heat, stir in the mint, cover, and let cool for 1 hour. Line a sieve with cheesecloth (muslin), strain the syrup through the sieve into a sealable jar, cover, and refrigerate. (The syrup can be prepared up to 1 week in advance.)

When ready to serve, fill 12 highball glasses with ice. Add 2 tablespoons of the ginger syrup and 1 tablespoon of the crystallized ginger to each glass. Fill with tonic water, stir, garnish with a lime slice, and serve.

Serves 12

GINGER SYRUP

375 ml (12 fl oz) water

375 g (12 oz) sugar

500 g (1 lb) fresh ginger, peeled
and grated

1 vanilla pod, split lengthwise

4 whole cloves

30 g (1 oz) fresh mint leaves

Ice cubes

12 tablespoons (140 g/4$^{1}/_{2}$ oz) chopped
crystallized ginger

3 litres (3 qt) tonic water

12 lime slices

Sesame Seed Puffs

1 pack (530 g/17 oz) frozen
puff pastry, thawed according
to pack directions

3 tablespoons Asian sesame oil

2 tablespoons white sesame seeds

1 tablespoon black sesame seeds

1 tablespoon sea salt

Whether served warm from the oven or at room temperature, these flavourful bite-sized puffs are a welcome alternative to store-bought cocktail crackers and take only minutes to prepare.

Position a rack in the middle of the oven and a second rack in the upper third and preheat to 200°C (400°F). Line two 30 by 43 cm (12 by 17 in) baking sheets with greaseproof paper.

On a lightly floured work surface, unfold 1 sheet of the puff pastry and brush the top surface with $1^1/_2$ tablespoons of the sesame oil. Using a fluted pastry cutter, cut the pastry sheet into 16 squares, each about 5 cm (2 in) square. Without moving the squares, cut each square in half on the diagonal into 2 triangles, for a total of 32 triangles. Sprinkle the top surface with 1 tablespoon of the white sesame seeds, $1^1/_2$ teaspoons of the black sesame seeds, and $1^1/_2$ teaspoons of the sea salt.

Separate the triangles and using a spatula transfer them to the baking sheets, spacing them evenly. Bake until golden brown and nicely puffed, about 16 minutes. After the first 8 minutes, switch the baking sheets between the racks and rotate them 180 degrees. Transfer the sesame seed puffs to a wire rack and let them cool for at least 5 minutes before serving. (The puffs can be baked up to 1 day in advance, cooled to room temperature, and stored in an airtight container. Recrisp in a 230°C/450°F oven for 3 minutes before serving.)

While the first batch is baking, prepare the second sheet of puff pastry, using the remaining sesame oil, sesame seeds, and sea salt. Let the baking sheets cool between the two bakings.

To serve, arrange the puffs on a serving tray lined with a cloth napkin or present them in bowls placed on the bar.

Makes 64 pieces; serves 10-12

CURRIED CHICKEN AND MANGO COCKTAIL TARTLETS

Naan, India's classic flat bread, forms the base of these savoury snacks. You can purchase the breads from Indian restaurants and speciality-food markets; pitta bread makes a fine substitute. Plan to make the chicken topping up to one day in advance, cover, and refrigerate.

Preheat the oven to 150°C (300°F). Cut each naan bread into 18 irregularly shaped 5 cm (2 in) pieces. Arrange them on 2 rimmed baking sheets in a single layer. Toast until brittle and lightly browned, about 15 minutes. Let them cool to room temperature and store in an airtight container until ready to serve or up to 1 day.

Put the chicken breasts in a shallow saucepan and add the coconut milk, bay leaf, peppercorns, and water. Bring to a simmer over medium-high heat, reduce the heat to low, cover partially, and poach for 10 minutes. Remove from the heat and let the chicken cool to room temperature in the liquid.

Remove the chicken from the poaching liquid and discard the liquid. Working with 1 chicken breast at a time on a cutting board, and using 2 forks, shred the chicken. Transfer to a bowl and add the shredded coconut, currants, celery, curry powder, mayonnaise, and yogurt. Season to taste with salt and pepper. Cover and refrigerate until ready to use or up to 1 day.

Stand the mango on one of its narrow sides on a cutting board. Using a sharp knife, cut slightly off centre, slicing off all the flesh from one side of the stone in a single piece. Repeat on the other side. Cut both pieces in half lengthwise and remove the skin. Cut the quarters crosswise into thin slices.

When ready to serve, top each naan toast with about 1 tablespoon of the curried chicken. Garnish with a mango slice and some chopped peanuts. Arrange on a serving tray lined with a tropical leaf or cloth napkin. Serve at once.

Makes 36 tartlets; serves 10-12

2 onion, garlic, or other savoury naan breads, 30 cm (12 ins) in diameter

2 boneless, skinless chicken breast halves

1 can (470 ml/15 fl oz) coconut milk

1 bay leaf

1 teaspoon black peppercorns

250 ml (8 fl oz) water

30 g (1 oz) unsweetened shredded dried coconut

45 g (1 1/2 oz) dried currants

2 celery stalks, finely chopped

1 tablespoon curry powder

2 tablespoons mayonnaise

2 tablespoons whole-milk yogurt

Salt and freshly ground pepper

1 firm but ripe mango

45 g (1 1/2 oz) chopped dry-roasted peanuts

Beef Kebabs with Basil-Pesto Dipping Sauce

MARINADE

80 ml (3 fl oz) Asian sesame oil

2 tablespoons rice vinegar

2 tablespoons soy sauce

1 tablespoon peeled and grated fresh ginger

2 teaspoons Thai-style green curry paste

1 kg (2 lb) skirt steak, in 1 piece

DIPPING SAUCE

45 g (1^1/$_2$ oz) tightly packed fresh basil leaves

45 g (1^1/$_2$ oz) tightly packed fresh coriander leaves

45 g (1^1/$_2$ oz) tightly packed fresh mint leaves

1 small green serrano chilli, seeded

2 cloves garlic

3 tablespoons Thai fish sauce

3 tablespoons fresh lime juice

155 g (5 oz) crunchy peanut butter

36 wooden skewers

3 spring onions, including tender green tops, thinly sliced on the diagonal

45 g (1^1/$_2$ oz) chopped dry-roasted peanuts

Paprika for garnish (optional)

If you make these kebabs and dipping sauce in advance, plan to remove both from the refrigerator 30 minutes before cooking and serving, so that the meat cooks evenly and the dipping sauce is creamy.

To make the marinade, stir together the sesame oil, vinegar, soy sauce, ginger, and green curry paste in a shallow baking dish. Set aside.

Trim the narrow end pieces off the skirt steak, so that you are left with a rectangular piece. Wrap in cling film and place flat in the freezer for 30 minutes. (This will facilitate the slicing of the meat.) Slice the steak against the grain on the diagonal into 36 slices each 6 mm (^{1}/$_4$ in) wide. Add the steak to the marinade and cover with cling film. Refrigerate for at least 30 minutes or up to 1 day.

To make the dipping sauce, in a food processor, combine the basil, coriander, mint, chilli, garlic, fish sauce, lime juice, and peanut butter and process until smooth. Transfer to a small serving bowl, cover with cling film, and refrigerate until 30 minutes before serving. (The dipping sauce can be made up to 1 day in advance.)

Soak the wooden skewers in water to cover in a shallow baking dish for 30 minutes and then drain. Position a rack 15 cm (6 in) from the heat source and preheat the grill.

Remove the beef slices from the marinade and drain well. Weave 1 slice of beef onto each skewer. Place the kebabs on rimmed baking sheets, spacing them evenly. (The beef can be kebabed 1 day in advance and stored in the refrigerator. Bring to room temperature to continue.)

Grill until cooked through, about 4 minutes, turning them once after the first 2 minutes.

To serve, place the bowl of dipping sauce and the kebabs on a large platter. Sprinkle the green onions and peanuts over the kebabs. Top with a sprinkle of paprika, if desired. Serve at once.

Makes 36 kebabs; serves 10-12

Prawn, Cantaloupe, and Fresh Herb Kebabs

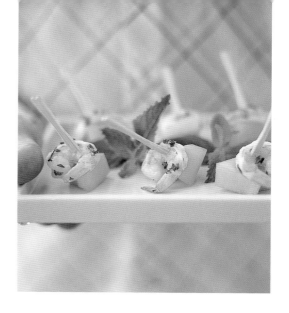

Cubes of sweet cantaloupe are paired with marinated prawns for a passed hors d'oeuvre that is unique and easy to prepare. Look for medium-sized prawns, which are just the right size for a satisfying bite.

In a bowl large enough to accommodate the prawns, stir together the coconut cream, fish sauce, lime juice, sesame oil, chives, chopped mint, and chilli. Set aside.

Bring a large pot of salted water to a boil over high heat. Add the prawns and cook until they turn pink and begin to curl, about 2 minutes. Using a slotted spoon, transfer the prawns to the bowl holding the coconut cream mixture and toss to coat evenly. allow to cool to room temperature, cover with cling film, and refrigerate for at least 2 hours or up to 8 hours.

Cut the cantaloupe half into 6 wedges. Working with 1 wedge at a time, remove the rind and cut the wedge into 6 equal pieces. You should have a total of 36 cubes of cantaloupe, each about 2 cm ($^3/_4$ in) wide.

Soak 36 wooden skewers in water to cover in a shallow baking dish for 30 minutes and then drain. Remove the prawns from the refrigerator and drain in a colander. To assemble the kebabs, thread 1 prawn and 1 piece of cantaloupe onto each skewer. Place the kebabs in a single layer on a rimmed baking sheet, cover with cling film, and refrigerate until ready to serve. (The prawns can be kebabed up to 4 hours in advance.)

To serve, arrange the kebabs down the centre of a narrow platter or tray, positioning them so that the kebab ends are easy to grasp. Garnish the platter with mint sprigs.

Makes 36 kebabs; serves 10-12

2 tablespoons coconut cream, scooped from the top of an unshaken can of coconut milk

1 tablespoon Thai fish sauce

2 teaspoons fresh lime juice

1 teaspoon Asian sesame oil

2 tablespoons snipped fresh chives

2 tablespoons chopped fresh mint, plus sprigs for garnish

1 small red chilli, seeded and minced

500 g (1 lb) medium prawns, peeled and deveined (36 prawns)

$^1/_2$ small cantaloupe melon

ASSORTED FRUIT SORBET SHOTS

500 ml each (16 fl oz) assorted sorbets such as coconut, mango, and kiwifruit

Diced fruits such as mango, banana, and kiwifruit for garnish

Pass small scoops of ready-made tropical fruit sorbets at the end of the evening. Guests will enjoy the cool mix of refreshing flavours, and something sweet will signal that the evening is coming to a close.

Select 42 shot glasses or small paper cups. Using a small ice-cream scoop about 4 cm ($1^{1}/_{2}$ in) in diameter, fill each glass with a scoop of sorbet. Place the glasses on a tray in the freezer until ready to serve, or up to 1 day in advance.

To serve, place a miniature wooden ice cream spoon or demitasse spoon in each glass. Garnish each serving with a few pieces of fruit. Arrange on 1 or 2 trays.

Makes 42 shots; serves 10-12

FAMILY REUNION BBQ

HOSTING AND SERVING TIPS

- Rent folding wooden chairs to accommodate everyone comfortably.

- Decorate the table with candles set in hurricane lamps or tall vases, alternating with tumblers or short vases holding a single bloom, such as a hydrangea or zinnia.

- If possible, allow access on both sides of the buffet table to help traffic flow more smoothly.

- Set the buffet, beverage, and dessert tables in shady spots; dress with linens, flowers, and candles that match the dining table.

- Set up a separate kids' table with unbreakable glasses and plates.

- For wine, serve a Côtes du Rhône for a red and a Sauvignon Blanc for a white.

MENU

Honeydew and Mint Agua Fresca

Classic Margaritas

•

*Sliced Tomatoes with Avocado,
Red Onion, and Parsley*

*Roasted Potato Salad
with Spring Onion Dressing*

Grilled Tomatillo Chicken Fajitas

*Grilled Corn on the Cob with
Chipotle Butter and Lime*

•

Ice-Cream Sundae Bar

WORK PLAN

UP TO 1 DAY IN ADVANCE

Make the salsa for the fajitas and
marinate the chicken

Prepare the corn

Make the dressing for the potato salad

UP TO 4 HOURS IN ADVANCE

Prepare the potato salad

Make the agua fresca

Slice the tomatoes and onion

Set up the sundae bar

JUST BEFORE SERVING

Finish the tomato salad

Grill the chicken and the corn

Assemble the fajitas

Mix the margaritas

Fill the sundae bar

SETTING UP A SUNDAE BAR

Fun for the guests and easy for the host, a self-service ice-cream bar is perfect for a crowd that includes kids. Set out bowls of toppings on trays in the kitchen ahead of time for quick last-minute setup.

assemble an assortment of bowls filled with topping ingredients, such as berries, small biscuits, nuts, maraschino cherries, sprinkles, and whipped cream.

fill squirt bottles with store-bought syrups, such as chocolate, caramel, and strawberry. Write the names of the syrups on colourful labels and attach to the bottles.

set ice-cream containers in ice-filled tubs. Wrap each tub with a dish towel or large cloth napkin and secure with a clothes peg. Arrange bowls, cones, and spoons alongside.

Honeydew and Mint Agua Fresca

This easy Latin drink of sweetened crushed fruit mixed with sparkling water is a nice alternative to soft drinks.

Cut the honeydew melons in half and remove and discard the seeds. Using a metal spoon, scoop out the flesh into a large bowl. Working in batches, purée the honeydew melon in a blender or food processor. As each batch is finished, transfer it to another large bowl. Add the lemon juice, sugar, and mint leaves to the purée and stir to combine until the sugar is dissolved. Cover and set aside at room temperature for at least 1 hour or up to 4 hours to blend the flavours.

When ready to serve, pour the melon mixture through a medium-mesh sieve into a large jug or jar. Add the sparkling water, lemon slices, and ice and stir well. Pour or ladle into glasses and garnish each glass with a mint sprig.

Serves 10-12

2 honeydew melons, about
6 kg (12 lb) total weight

Juice of 4 lemons

185 g (6 oz) sugar

30 g (1 oz) crushed fresh
mint leaves

750 ml (24 fl oz) sparkling water, chilled

3 lemons, thinly sliced

Ice cubes

10-12 fresh mint sprigs for garnish

Classic Margaritas

Blended or on the rocks, salt or no salt—margaritas can vary. But always start with good tequila, fresh lime juice, and a quality liqueur.

Select 8 margarita glasses. Spread a layer of salt on a small, flat plate. Working with 1 glass at a time, run a lime wedge around the rim of the glass to moisten it and then dip the rim into the salt to coat it evenly. Put the glass in the freezer to chill for at least 15 minutes. Repeat with the remaining glasses, using the same lime wedge to moisten all the rims.

When ready to serve, mix the drinks in 2 batches: Fill a blender half full with ice. Add half of the tequila, half of the lime juice, half of the orange liqueur, and half of the frozen limeade concentrate. Purée until well blended. Divide the mixture evenly among 4 of the chilled glasses. Garnish each glass with a lime wedge. Serve at once. Repeat to make the second batch.

Serves 8

Sea salt for coating the glass rims

9 lime wedges

Ice cubes

375 ml (12 fl oz) 100% agave tequila

250 ml (8 fl oz) fresh lime juice

125 ml (4 fl oz) orange liqueur,
preferably Cointreau or Grand Marnier

250 ml (8 fl oz) frozen limeade
concentrate, kept frozen

Sliced Tomatoes with Avocado, Red Onion, and Parsley

3 avocados, halved, stoned, peeled, and thinly sliced

Juice of 1 lemon

8 assorted tomatoes, thinly sliced

1 small red onion, thinly sliced

60 ml (2 fl oz) fruity extra-virgin olive oil

Sea salt and freshly ground pepper

2 tablespoons coarsely chopped fresh flat-leaf (Italian) parsley

To maximise your prep time, slice the tomatoes and onion a few hours in advance, arrange them on a platter, cover with plastic wrap, and refrigerate; finish the salad just before serving.

In a bowl, toss the avocado slices with the lemon juice. On a large platter, arrange the tomato slices, slightly overlapping, in a single layer. Scatter the onion and avocado slices over the top. Drizzle with the olive oil and any lemon juice that is left from the avocados. Sprinkle with salt, pepper, and the parsley. Serve at once.

Roasted Potato Salad with Spring Onion Dressing

1.5 kg (3 lb) baby potatoes, each about 2.5 cm (1 in) in diameter

3 tablespoons olive oil

1 tablespoon sea salt

DRESSING

15 g (1/2 oz) fresh coriander leaves, plus sprigs for garnish

3 spring onions, including tender green tops, chopped

1 clove garlic, chopped

125 g (4 oz) sour cream

60 ml (2 fl oz) mayonnaise

4 teaspoons red wine vinegar

4 teaspoons Dijon mustard

Sea salt and freshly ground pepper

With no peeling or cutting needed, this potato salad is fast to prepare. Roasting produces potatoes with crispy skin and a creamy interior. (See photograph on page 91.)

Preheat the oven to 200°C (400°F). Put the potatoes on a rimmed baking sheet, drizzle with the olive oil, sprinkle with the salt, and toss to coat evenly. Roast, tossing every 15 minutes, until the skins are crisp and golden brown, about 45 minutes. Let cool.

Meanwhile, make the dressing: In a food processor or blender, combine the coriander leaves, spring onions, garlic, sour cream, mayonnaise, vinegar, and mustard and process until smooth. Season to taste with salt and pepper, cover, and refrigerate until ready to use. (The dressing can be prepared up to 1 day in advance and refrigerated.)

To serve, put the cooled potatoes in a serving bowl, add the dressing, and toss to coat. Garnish with the coriander sprigs. Serve at once, or cover and refrigerate for up to 4 hours.

Each recipe serves 10-12

GRILLED TOMATILLO CHICKEN FAJITAS

Mexican crema, *a thin cultured cream, can be found at Mexican food stores and some supermarkets. Sour cream thinned with single cream can be substituted.*

To make the tomatillo salsa, position a rack 10 cm (4 in) from the heat source and preheat the grill. Put the tomatillos, chillis, garlic, and onion on a rimmed baking sheet. Sprinkle with the cumin, oregano, and salt. Drizzle with the olive oil and toss to combine. Grill, turning once, until the vegetables are soft and lightly charred, about 8 minutes. Allow to cool to room temperature, then transfer to a food processor and add the lime juice and coriander. Purée until almost smooth, cover and refrigerate until ready to use or for up to 2 days.

Rinse the chicken breasts and pat dry with paper towels. Arrange in a single layer in a shallow baking dish and sprinkle with the salt and pepper. Pour 1 cup 250 ml (8 fl oz) of the salsa over the chicken and toss until evenly coated. Cover and refrigerate for at least 2 hours or up to 1 day. Transfer the remaining salsa to a small serving bowl, cover, and refrigerate until ready to serve.

Prepare a charcoal or gas grill for direct grilling over medium-high heat. Oil the grill rack and position it about 15 cm (6 in) from the heat source. Rub the pepper halves and spring onions with the olive oil.

Grill the pepper halves and spring onions, turning frequently, until tender and lightly charred, 5-6 minutes for the peppers and 2-3 minutes for the onions. Slice the peppers into thin strips and cut the onions on the diagonal into 5 cm (2 in) pieces. Wrap in aluminium foil to keep warm.

Remove the chicken from the marinade, discarding the marinade. Grill, turning once, until opaque throughout, about 20 minutes total. Cut the chicken on the diagonal into slices 12 mm ($^1/_2$ in) thick, capturing any juices.

Arrange the chicken, peppers, and spring onions on a warmed platter. Drizzle with any carving juices, the *crema*, and a little of the reserved salsa. Serve accompanied by the tortillas and salsa.

Serves 10-12

ROASTED TOMATILLO SALSA

1 lb (500 g) tomatillos, husks removed, rinsed and quartered

2 chillis, seeded and coarsely chopped

2 cloves garlic

1 small white onion, quartered

1 teaspoon ground cumin

1 teaspoon dried oregano

$^1/_2$ teaspoon sea salt

2 tablespoons olive oil

Juice of 2 limes

10 g ($^1/_3$ oz) fresh coriander leaves

1.5 kg (3 lb) boneless, skinless chicken breasts

1 teaspoon sea salt

1 teaspoon freshly ground pepper

2 red peppers (capsicums), halved, seeded, and stemmed

2 yellow peppers (capsicums), halved, seeded, and stemmed

6 spring onions, roots and top 7.5 cm (3 in) of green tops trimmed

3 tablespoons olive oil

175 ml (5 $^1/_2$ fl oz) *crema*

12 flour tortillas, 20 cm (8 in) in diameter, warmed

GRILLED CORN ON THE COB WITH CHIPOTLE BUTTER AND LIME

185 g (6 oz) unsalted butter,
at room temperature

1 tablespoon chipotle chilli powder

Grated zest of 2 limes

2 teaspoons sea salt

12 ears of corn, husks intact

3 limes, quartered

Corn on the cob becomes something special when rubbed with a seasoned butter and grilled in its husks. The evening before the party, prepare the ears of corn up to the point where they are ready to be grilled. Not only will you have fewer things to take care of the next day, but the corn will absorb the sweet, smoky flavour of the chipotle butter overnight.

In a bowl, using a wooden spoon, mix the butter, chilli powder, lime zest, and salt into a smooth paste. Set aside at room temperature for 30 minutes to blend the flavours.

Working with 1 ear of corn at a time, peel down the husks and remove the silk strands, making sure that the husks remain attached at the base of the ear. Using a pastry brush or small rubber spatula, brush or spread 1 tablespoon of the chipotle butter evenly over the ear of corn. Fold the husks back up over the ear so that it is completely enclosed. Repeat with the remaining ears of corn. (The corn can be prepared up to 1 day in advance. Cover with cling film, and refrigerate, then bring to room temperature before grilling.)

Prepare a charcoal or gas grill for direct grilling over medium-high heat. Position a grill rack about 15 cm (6 in) from the heat source.

Grill the ears of corn, turning often so that they cook evenly, until the kernels are tender and the husks are charred all over, 10-15 minutes. Arrange the corn on a platter with the lime quarters on top. Let each guest unwrap an ear of corn and squeeze a little lime juice over it before eating.

Serves 10-12

Ice-Cream Sundae Bar

Both kids and adults will have fun making their favourite soda fountain speciality, whether it's a favourite fruit punch float, a classic banana split, or a traditional sundae topped with whipped cream and a cherry. Have plenty of ice or dry ice on hand to keep the ice creams well chilled.

Transfer the store-bought sauces to squirt bottles and label each bottle. Place the blueberries, raspberries, maraschino cherries, chocolate chips, toffee-bar pieces, cookies, and nuts in small bowls for toppings. Transfer the whipped cream to a small serving bowl.

Pack the whipped cream, ice creams, and ginger beer on ice so that they remain cold, and place within easy reach of guests. Set out the sauces, toppings, bananas, and waffle cones. Let guests create their own ice-cream confections.

Serves 10-12

375 ml (12 fl oz) store-bought chocolate sauce

375 ml (12 fl oz) store-bought caramel sauce

375 ml (12 fl oz) store-bought strawberry sauce

250 g (8 oz) blueberries

250 g (8 oz) raspberries

185 g (6 oz) maraschino cherries

185 g (6 oz) miniature chocolate chips

155 g (5 oz) broken toffee-bar pieces

90 g (3 oz) whole small biscuits or biscuit pieces

125 g (4 oz) walnuts or sliced (flaked) almonds, toasted

500 ml (16 fl oz) double cream, whipped

1 litre (32 fl oz) vanilla ice cream

1 litre (32 fl oz) chocolate ice cream

1 litre (32 fl oz) strawberry ice cream

6 bottles (375 ml each/12 fl oz) old-fashioned ginger beer, chilled

3 bananas, unpeeled

12 waffle ice-cream cones

EQUIPMENT

3 plastic squirt bottles

Assorted small glass bowls

2 bags (10 kg /20 lb each) ice

Ice-cream scoops

Assorted soda fountain glasses

Soda fountain spoons

Straws

MIDWEEK GRILL

HOSTING AND SERVING TIPS

- For predinner nibbles, set out olives, capers, and salted pistachios or almonds.

- To keep the look casual, use place mats instead of tablecloths and serve wine in decanters.

- Place a single large blossom, such as a magnolia or a gardenia, in a plain footed bowl for an easy centrepiece.

- Offer bread sticks in a long olive dish lined with a cloth napkin.

- For wine, serve a Bordeaux or Zinfandel for a red and a Viognier or a white Burgundy for a white.

MENU

Sparkling Wine Cocktails

·

*Mâche, Radish, Blue Cheese,
and Sugared Pecan Salad*

Grilled Seasoned Halibut

Potato Fennel Purée

Grilled Courgettes and Broad Beans with Sea Salt

·

*Sautéed Cherries over
Chocolate Chip Ice Cream*

WORK PLAN

UP TO 1 WEEK IN ADVANCE

Toast the sugared pecans

UP TO 4 HOURS IN ADVANCE

Make the vinaigrette for the salad

Season the fish

JUST BEFORE SERVING

Mix the wine cocktails

Make the potato purée

Grill the vegetables and fish

Assemble and dress the salad

Prepare the dessert

SPARKLING WINE COCKTAILS

Chilled Champagne cocktails are a special but easy way to start an evening with friends. Use a medium-priced dry Champagne or other sparkling wine. You can substitute another fruit-flavoured liqueur for the melon liqueur, such as peach, apple, or pear.

Put 4 tall, narrow glasses in the freezer to chill for at least 15 minutes.

When ready to serve, pour 1 tablespoon of the melon liqueur into each chilled glass. Slowly fill the glasses with Champagne and garnish each with a twist of orange zest and a mint sprig.

Serves 4

4 tablespoons (60 ml/2 fl oz) chilled melon liqueur

1 bottle (750 ml/24 fl oz) chilled Champagne or other sparkling wine

4 orange zest twists

4 small fresh mint sprigs

Mâche, Radish, Blue Cheese, and Sugared Pecan Salad

PECANS

60 g (2 oz) pecan halves

1 teaspoon sugar

1/4 teaspoon dry mustard

Pinch of cayenne pepper

VINAIGRETTE

1 shallot, finely chopped

80 ml (3 fl oz) olive oil

2 tablespoons red wine vinegar

1 teaspoon Dijon mustard

Sea salt and freshly ground black
pepper

1 pack (125 g/4 oz) mâche

8 radishes, thinly sliced

125 g (1/4 lb) blue cheese, crumbled

Mâche is a tender, nutty-flavoured salad leaf that is sold in ready-to-use bags in the produce section of many supermarkets. For a substitute, use a mixture of tender rocket and baby spinach leaves.
You can make the sugared pecans up to one week in advance and store in an airtight container at room temperature.

To prepare the pecans, preheat the oven to 180°C (350°F). Rinse the pecans in a sieve and set aside to drain. In a small bowl, combine the sugar, dry mustard, and cayenne and mix well. Add the pecans and toss until evenly coated. Spread the pecans on a nonstick rimmed baking sheet and toast in the oven until dark brown, about 10 minutes. Transfer the pecans to a plate, let them cool, and set aside.

To make the vinaigrette, in a small bowl, whisk together the shallot, olive oil, vinegar, and Dijon mustard. Season to taste with salt and black pepper. Let stand at room temperature for at least 30 minutes or up to 4 hours to blend the flavours.

To serve, combine the mâche leaves and radish slices in a salad bowl. Drizzle with the vinaigrette and toss until evenly coated. Top with the blue cheese and the pecans. Serve at once.

Serves 4

GRILLED SEASONED HALIBUT

Serve these simply grilled fillets on individual plates atop a mound of the Potato Fennel Purée (below); drizzle with orange-infused olive oil.

Brush the halibut fillets with the olive oil to coat completely. In a small bowl, stir together the chervil, fennel seeds, orange zest, salt, and pepper. Sprinkle the mixture over the halibut fillets, distributing it evenly so that all sides are seasoned. Transfer the fillets to a shallow baking dish, cover, and refrigerate for up to 4 hours. Bring to room temperature 15 minutes before grilling.

Prepare a charcoal or gas grill for direct grilling over medium-high heat. Oil the grill rack and position it about 15 cm (6 in) from the heat source.

Grill the halibut fillets, turning once, until opaque throughout, 3–4 minutes on each side. Garnish with chervil and serve at once.

Serves 4

4 skinless halibut fillets, each about 185 g (6 oz) and 2.5 cm (1 in) thick

60 ml (2 fl oz) olive oil

1 tablespoon chopped fresh chervil, plus extra for garnish

1 teaspoon fennel seeds, crushed

Grated zest of $1/2$ orange

1 teaspoon sea salt

$1/2$ teaspoon freshly ground pepper

POTATO FENNEL PURÉE

Here is a light alternative to traditional mashed potatoes. The addition of mayonnaise enriches the flavour and keeps the purée creamy. The purée can be prepared up to 30 minutes before serving, covered, and reheated.

In a large pot over medium-high heat, warm the olive oil. Add the fennel and sauté until translucent and golden, about 15 minutes. Add the stock, potatoes, and 1 teaspoon salt. Reduce the heat to maintain a simmer, cover, and cook until the potatoes are soft when pierced with a knife, about 30 minutes.

Drain the potatoes and fennel in a colander, return to the pot, and immediately mash with a potato masher. Add the butter and slowly pour in the milk while stirring with a wooden spoon. Add the mayonnaise and continue to stir until light and creamy. Season to taste with salt and pepper.

Serves 4

2 tablespoons olive oil

2 fennel bulbs, quartered, cored, and finely diced

625 ml (20 fl oz) chicken stock

1 kg (2 lb) potatoes, peeled and quartered

Sea salt

2 tablespoons unsalted butter

125 ml (4 fl oz) whole milk, heated

2 tablespoons mayonnaise

Freshly ground pepper

GRILLED COURGETTES AND BROAD BEANS WITH SEA SALT

Use a quality salt to bring out the flavour of grilled vegetables. Sea salt is best, preferably fleur de sel, *harvested along the Brittany coast of France. Look for a selection of sea salts at speciality-food stores.*

16 young, tender broad bean pods

3 medium courgettes, trimmed and sliced lengthwise

3 tablespoons olive oil

1 teaspoon sea salt, plus more for serving

1/2 teaspoon freshly ground fine pepper

Fruity extra-virgin olive oil for drizzling

Freshly ground coarse pepper for serving

Prepare a charcoal or gas grill for direct grilling over medium-high heat. Position a grill rack about 15 cm (6 in) from the heat source.

Rub the broad bean pods and courgette slices with the olive oil and season with the 1 teaspoon salt and the fine pepper.

Arrange the broad bean pods and courgette slices on the grill rack and grill, turning often, until evenly charred and the courgette slices are tender, about 5 minutes.

Transfer to a warmed platter, drizzle with extra-virgin olive oil, and sprinkle with salt and coarse pepper. Allow each guest to remove the beans from their pods and then squeeze the beans from their tough skins.

Serves 4

Sautéed Cherries over Chocolate Chip Ice Cream

Use firm, sweet cherries, which will hold their shape when cooked. If fresh cherries are unavailable, substitute frozen cherries that have been thoroughly thawed and drained.

In a nonreactive bowl, toss together the cherries and lemon juice. Set aside.

In a large frying pan over medium heat, melt the butter. Add the cherries and brown sugar and sauté until the cherries are soft and the sugar is caramelized, about 5 minutes. Remove from the heat and swirl in the kirsch.

To serve, scoop the ice cream into individual bowls or stemmed glasses. Top each serving with an equal amount of the warm cherries and drizzle some of the pan juices over the top. Serve at once.

Serves 4

375 g (12 oz) stoned cherries

Juice of 1/2 lemon

4 tablespoons (60 g / 2 oz) unsalted butter

60 g (2 oz) firmly packed light brown sugar

2 tablespoons kirsch

500 ml (16 fl oz) chocolate chip ice cream

MEDITERRANEAN FEAST

HOSTING AND
SERVING TIPS

- Layer linens in neutral earth tones.
  Put place mats or napkins over
  the tablecloth, and top each plate
  with a folded napkin.

- Serve olive oil and vinegar in glass
  bottles with spouts for easy pouring
  at the table.

- To add a cheese course, drizzle honey
  on pecorino slices and walnuts.

- For wine, serve a well-chilled White
  Shiraz (or Syrah Rosé) for a rosé;
  a light Pinot Noir for a red; and a
  Vernaccia for a white.

MENU

Grilled Flat Bread with Two Spreads

•

*Lamb and Vegetable Brochettes
with Mint Gremolata*

*Cucumber Ribbons with Tomatoes,
Ricotta Salata, and Olives*

*Orzo Salad with Artichoke Hearts,
Pine Nuts, and Sultanas*

•

Apricot Pistachio Tart

Spice-Infused Iced Coffee

WORK PLAN

UP TO 1 DAY IN ADVANCE

Make the spreads

Marinate the lamb

Prepare the dressing, orzo, and
artichokes separately

Make the infused coffee

UP TO 4 HOURS IN ADVANCE

Marinate the vegetables

Make the *gremolata*

Prepare and bake the tart

JUST BEFORE SERVING

Grill the flat breads and the brochettes

Make the cucumber salad

Toss the orzo salad

HERB CENTREPIECE

Everyday elements, such as sprigs of greenery and candles, can help set a scene. Here, they decorate a table dressed with neutral-toned linens to evoke the mood of a relaxed supper in a Mediterranean garden.

gather greenery, such as olive branches or sprigs of tarragon or sage, rosemary topiaries, unscented pillar candles, small plates, and hurricane lamps.

place the topiaries in a line running down the centre of the table, leaving space between them. Put the candles on plates between the topiaries.

scatter the olive sprays along the table, and tuck one into each napkin. Just before the meal, light the candles and cover them with the hurricane chimneys.

GRILLED FLAT BREAD WITH TWO SPREADS

Arrange the grilled flat breads and spreads on a board and pass them as an appetizer. If you are pressed for time, you can substitute store-bought houmous, tapenade (olive spread), or baba ganoush (aubergine dip). Both spreads can be prepared up to one day in advance and refrigerated.

Prepare a charcoal or gas grill for direct grilling over medium-high heat. Oil the grill rack and position it about 15 cm (6 in) from the heat source. Preheat the oven to 95°C (200°F).

Lightly brush the flat breads with olive oil and grill, turning once, until lightly toasted and warmed through, about 1 minute on each side. Remove from the grill and tear each flat bread into 6 pieces. Wrap in aluminium foil and keep warm in the oven until ready to serve.

To make the roasted pepper spread, in a food processor, combine the roasted red peppers, olives, capers, anchovies, garlic, and bread and pulse to blend. Stream in the extra-virgin olive oil and lemon juice and pulse until almost smooth. Transfer to an airtight container and refrigerate until ready to serve. Remove the spread from the refrigerator 30 minutes before serving to bring to room temperature. Mound into a deep serving bowl.

To make the white bean spread, in a food processor, combine the beans, parsley, oregano, basil, green onions, garlic, and red pepper flakes and pulse to blend. Stream in the extra-virgin olive oil and lemon juice and pulse 2 or 3 times until the olive oil and lemon juice are incorporated. The spread should be smooth but still have some texture. Season to taste with salt and black pepper. Transfer to an airtight container and refrigerate until ready to serve. Remove the spread from the refrigerator 30 minutes before serving to bring to room temperature. Transfer to a serving bowl and scatter the feta cheese and parsley on the top.

Place the spreads alongside the warm flat breads and serve at once.

Serves 8

---

12 Middle Eastern-style flat breads or pitta breads

2 tablespoons olive oil

ROASTED PEPPER, OLIVE, AND CAPER SPREAD

1 jar (375 g/12 oz) roasted red peppers (capsicums), drained

60 g (2 oz) stoned mixed olives

60 g (2 oz) capers, drained

375 g (12 oz) anchovy fillets, drained

2 cloves garlic

250 g (1/2 lb) white bread, crusts removed and bread cut into 2.5 cm (1 in) cubes

125 ml (4 fl oz) extra-virgin olive oil

1 tablespoon fresh lemon juice

WHITE BEAN AND HERB SPREAD

2 cans (470 g/15 oz) each cannellini beans, rinsed and drained

10 g (1/3 oz) chopped fresh flat-leaf (Italian) parsley, plus extra for garnish

2 tablespoons *each* chopped fresh oregano and basil

3 spring onions, including tender green tops, chopped

1 clove garlic, chopped

Pinch of red pepper flakes

60 ml (2 fl oz) extra-virgin olive oil

3 tablespoons fresh lemon juice

Salt and freshly ground black pepper

60 g (2 oz) feta cheese, crumbled

Lamb and Vegetable Brochettes with Mint Gremolata

MINT GREMOLATA

2 tablespoons chopped fresh mint

2 tablespoons chopped fresh flat-leaf (Italian) parsley

2 cloves garlic, minced

1 tablespoon grated lemon zest

250 ml (8 fl oz) extra-virgin olive oil

125 ml (4 fl oz) dry red wine

2 tablespoons tomato purée

2 tablespoons balsamic vinegar

3 tablespoons chopped fresh rosemary

2 cloves garlic, minced

2 teaspoons sea salt

1 teaspoon freshly ground pepper

1 kg (2 lb) piece trimmed boneless leg of lamb, cut into 3 cm (1 1/4 in) cubes

2 green courgettes, cut into rounds 2.5 cm (1 in) thick

2 yellow courgettes, cut into rounds 2.5 cm (1 in) thick

2 slender aubergines, cut into rounds 2.5 cm (1 in) thick

2 large red onions, cut into 5 cm (2 in) pieces

16 sturdy woody rosemary branches, each about 25 cm (10 in) long, or wooden skewers

Make up a few extra vegetable brochettes if you know some of your guests don't eat meat. Always place the vegetable brochettes around the perimeter of the grill where the temperature is lower, so that they are done at the same time as the meat brochettes.

To make the *gremolata*, in a small bowl, mix together the mint, parsley, garlic, and lemon zest until well blended. Cover and refrigerate until ready to use. (The *gremolata* can be prepared up to 4 hours in advance.)

In a small bowl, whisk together the olive oil, wine, tomato purée, vinegar, rosemary, garlic, salt, and pepper until well blended. Put the lamb cubes in a large heavy-duty sealsble plastic bag. Put the courgettes, aubergines, and onion pieces in another bag. Divide the marinade evenly between the 2 bags. Press out any excess air, seal the bags, turn to coat the contents evenly with the marinade, and refrigerate. The lamb can marinate overnight but the vegetables should not marinate for more than 4 hours.

Strip the leaves off each rosemary branch, leaving a few leaves on the tip. Using a sharp knife, shape the other end to a sharp point. Soak the branches or skewers in water to cover in a shallow baking dish for 30 minutes and then drain. Prepare a charcoal or gas grill for direct grilling over medium-high heat. Oil the grill rack and position it about 15 cm (6 in) from the heat source.

Remove the lamb pieces from the marinade and discard the marinade. Thread onto 8 of the rosemary branches, making sure not to crowd them so they cook evenly. Thread the vegetables in an alternating pattern onto the remaining 8 rosemary branches. Reserve the vegetable marinade for basting. Place the lamb kebabs in the centre of the grill over the hottest part of the fire and the vegetable kebabs around them. Grill, turning and basting every few minutes, until the lamb is cooked through and the vegetables are tender and lightly charred, 10-12 minutes.

Arrange the kebabs on a warmed platter and sprinkle with the mint *gremolata*. Serve at once.

Serves 8

Cucumber Ribbons with Tomatoes, Ricotta Salata, and Olives

Cucumber ribbons require a little effort, but the end result makes for an unusual salad. Shavings of ricotta salata, *a dry, salted type of ricotta cheese, finish the presentation. Use crumbly feta as a substitute.*

Peel the cucumbers and cut in half lengthwise. Using a small metal spoon, scoop out the seeds (there will be very few) and discard them. Cut each half in half crosswise. Using a vegetable peeler or mandoline, cut the cucumbers lengthwise into ribbons about 3 mm ($^1/_8$ in) thick.

In a large salad bowl, toss together the cucumber ribbons and tomatoes. Mound them on a serving platter. Scatter the olives, cheese, and thyme over the top. Drizzle with the olive oil and vinegar and season to taste with salt and pepper. Serve at once.

Serves 8

2 cucumbers, about 1 kg (2 lb) total weight

3 vine-ripened tomatoes, seeded and diced

75 g (2$^1/_2$ oz) pitted olives, halved lengthwise

125 g ($^1/_4$ lb) *ricotta salata*, cut into shavings with a vegetable peeler

2 tablespoons chopped fresh thyme

3 tablespoons extra-virgin olive oil

1 tablespoon red wine vinegar

Sea salt and freshly ground pepper

Orzo Salad with Artichoke Hearts, Pine Nuts, and Sultanas

DRESSING

60 ml (2 fl oz) fresh lemon juice

1 tablespoon Dijon mustard

2 cloves garlic

15 g (½ oz) fresh basil leaves

125 ml (4 fl oz) olive oil

500 g (1 lb) orzo pasta

Olive oil

12 fresh baby artichokes, or 2 cans
(440 g/14 oz each) artichoke hearts,
rinsed

1 lemon, halved

140 g (4½ oz) sultanas

45 g (1½ oz) pine nuts, toasted

15 g (½ oz) fresh basil leaves,
julienned

3 spring onions, including tender green
tops, thinly sliced on the diagonal

Sea salt and freshly ground pepper

When tossed with the other components in this salad, the individual rice-shaped orzo pasta grains separate and absorb the flavourful dressing. The dressing, orzo, and artichokes can be prepared up to one day in advance and stored in individual airtight containers in the refrigerator; remove 30 minutes before serving and bring to room temperature.

To make the dressing, in a food processor, combine the lemon juice, mustard, garlic, basil, and olive oil and purée until smooth and emulsified. Transfer to a small bowl and set aside.

Bring a large pot three-quarters full of salted water to a boil over high heat. Add the orzo and cook according to the pack directions until al dente. Rinse well in cold water to remove any excess starch and drain in a colander. Transfer to a large bowl and toss lightly with a little olive oil to prevent the grains from sticking together.

If using fresh artichokes, trim the stems, leaving about 12 mm (½ in). Cut 12 mm (½ in) off the tops. Peel away the tough outer leaves until you reach the tender, pale green leaves. Cut each artichoke lengthwise into 6 wedges and rub them with the cut lemon halves. Bring a pot three-quarters full of salted water to a boil. Add the artichokes and cook until tender, about 14 minutes. Drain and allow to cool to room temperature. If using canned artichokes, drain and cut lengthwise into 6 wedges.

Add the artichokes, sultanas, pine nuts, basil, and spring onions to the bowl containing the orzo. Drizzle with the dressing and toss to coat evenly. Season to taste with salt and pepper. Transfer to a serving bowl and serve at once.

Serves 8

APRICOT PISTACHIO TART

You can quickly assemble this delicious seasonal fruit tart using store-bought pastry dough and fruit preserves. For an autumn variation, use 155 g (5 oz) cranberry preserves instead of apricot, and substitute walnuts and poached pear halves for the pistachios and apricots.

Remove 1 sheet of puff pastry from the pack and thaw in the refrigerator for 24-36 hours, or according to pack directions. Wrap the remaining sheet in plastic wrap and keep frozen for another use.

Preheat the oven to 200°C (400°F). Lightly butter a 25 cm (10 in) tart pan with a removable bottom.

On a lightly floured work surface, roll out the puff pastry sheet into a 28 cm (11 in) square. Drape the dough over the rolling pin and transfer it to the prepared tart pan. Trim off the corners and then gather any overhang and press it into the sides of the pan to form a rim that is even in thickness. Using a fork, prick the bottom and sides of the dough. Place the tart shell in the freezer for 15 minutes. Remove from the freezer and bake the unfilled tart shell until lightly golden, about 15 minutes.

While the tart shell is baking, in a bowl, toss the apricot halves together with the sugar and orange liqueur. Let stand to macerate at room temperature for 15 minutes.

To assemble the tart, spread the apricot preserves evenly over the bottom of the partially baked tart shell. Sprinkle the cinnamon, cardamom, and 4 tablespoons 30 g (1 oz) of the pistachios over the preserves. Arrange the apricot halves, cut sides down, in concentric circles over the preserves, and drizzle any of the juices remaining in the bowl over the surface. Sprinkle the remaining 2 tablespoons of pistachios over the top.

Bake the tart until the apricots are tender and the pastry is golden brown, 30-40 minutes. Remove from the oven and drizzle the honey over the top. Let it cool on a wire rack before slicing. (The tart can be prepared up to 4 hours in advance, cooled, tented with aluminium foil, and stored at room temperature.)

Serves 8

1 pack 530 g (17 oz) frozen puff pastry

10 apricots, halved and pitted

2 tablespoons sugar

1 tablespoon orange liqueur

155 g (5 oz) thick apricot preserves

1 teaspoon ground cinnamon

1/2 teaspoon ground cardamom

6 tablespoons 45 g (11/2 oz) chopped pistachios

2 tablespoons honey

SPICE-INFUSED ICED COFFEE

60 g (2 oz) instant espresso powder

500 ml (16 fl oz) boiling water

4 cardamom pods, slightly crushed

2 cinnamon sticks

Ice cubes

160 ml (5 fl oz) sweetened
condensed milk

A speciality iced-coffee drink offered at the end of the meal is a refreshing alternative to the usual cup of hot coffee. Here, the iced treat is flavoured with cardamom and cinnamon. The infused espresso will hold for up to three days, so make extra to keep on hand in the refrigerator.

In a small heatproof bowl, dissolve the espresso powder in the boiling water. Add the cardamom pods and cinnamon sticks to the bowl and let it stand until the liquid is cooled to room temperature, about 30 minutes. Drain and discard the cardamom pods and cinnamon sticks.

When ready to serve, working in two batches, fill a cocktail shaker half full with ice. Pour in half of the infused espresso and half of the condensed milk. Cover with the lid and shake vigorously for 1 minute. Strain into small tumblers. Serve at once. Repeat to make the second batch.

Serves 8

INDEX

ACKNOWLEDGEMENTS

WELDON OWEN wishes to thank the following individuals and organizations for their kind assistance: Desne Ahlers, Carrie Bradley, Ken DellaPenta, Sharon Silva, Steve Siegelman, Sarah Mattern, Renée Myers, Shadin Saah, Colin Wheatland, Simon Snellgrove, Shashona Burke, Sheana Butler, Julie Glavin, Reenie and Richard Benzinger, Skipper Cummings, Tina-Lise and David Curtis, and Belinda Levensohn.

GEORGE DOLESE would like to thank his associate, Elisabet der Nederlanden, for her contribution to the writing and styling of the recipes featured in this book – I am so lucky to be able to work with you; John Granen for joining us for a day at the beach and making our food look so good on film; Robin Turk for the beautiful table styling; editor Amy Marr for being our true recipe tester and making us smile with a big "yummm"; Nicky Collings for her humour and artistic eye; and Hannah Rahill and the staff at Weldon Owen for being such a loyal client. This book is dedicated to John and Tim, whose friendship, home, and lifestyle serve as a constant inspiration for my work.

PHOTO CREDITS

JIM FRANCO, all photography, except for the following:

JOHN GRANEN: Pages 13-31, and back cover image (centre)

ELLEN SILVERMAN: Front cover image

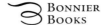

BONNIER BOOKS

Appledram Barns

Birdham Road

Chichester

West Sussex

PO20 7EQ

Bonnier Books edition

First published 2007

ISBN-13: 978-1-905825-20-2

Bonnier Books Website

www.bonnierbooks.co.uk

Printed in China

Jacket Images

Front cover: Family Reunion BBQ, page 86.

Back cover: Apple Limeade, page 41; Beachside Picnic Dinner, page 17; Mediterranean Feast, page 130.

THE ENTERTAINING SERIES.

Conceived and produced by Weldon Owen Inc.

814 Montgomery Street, San Francisco, CA 94133

Telephone: 415 291 0100 Fax: 415 291 8841

In Collaboration with Williams-Sonoma, Inc.

3250 Van Ness Avenue, San Francisco, CA 94109

WELDON OWEN INC.

Chief Executive Officer: John Owen

President and Chief Operating Officer: Terry Newell

Chief Financial Officer: Christine E. Munson

VP International Sales: Stuart Laurence

Creative Director: Gaye Allen

Publisher: Hannah Rahill

Associate Publisher: Amy Marr

Art Director: Nicky Collings

Design Consultant: Emma Boys

Designer: Rachel Lopez

Production Director: Chris Hemesath

Colour Manager: Teri Bell

Production and Reprint Coordinator: Todd Rechner

Associate Food Stylist: Elisabet der Nederlanden

Photographer's Assistants: Heidi Ladendorf, Daniel Weiner

Assistant Prop Stylists: Julie Maldonado, Sara Prentiss-Shaw, Pat Scott Spezzano